20 AND SOMETHING

D0862311

FRAMES
BARNA GROUP

20 AND SOMETHING
Have the Time of Your Life (And Figure It All Out Too)

DAVID H. KIM
RE/FRAME BY PHYLLIS TICKLE

ZONDERVAN®

ZONDERVAN

20 and Something
Copyright © 2013 by Barna Group

This title is also available as a Zondervan ebook.
Visit www.zondervan.com/ebooks.

This title is also available in a Zondervan audio edition.
Visit www.zondervan.fm.

Requests for information should be addressed to:

Zondervan, *Grand Rapids, Michigan 49530*

ISBN 978-0-310-43347-7 (softcover)

Published in association with the literary agency of The Fedd Agency, Inc,
401 Ranch Road 620 South, Suite 350c, Austin, TX 78734.

Cover design and interior graphics: Amy Duty
Interior design: Kate Mulvaney

Printed in the United States of America

13 14 15 16 17 18 /DCI/ 18 17 16 15 14 13 12 11 10 9 8 7 6 5 4 3 2 1

CONTENTS

WHY YOU NEED FRAMES

··

These days, you probably find yourself with less time than ever.

Everything seems like it's moving at a faster pace—except your ability to keep up.

Somehow, you are weighed down with more obligations than you have ever had before.

Life feels more complicated. More complex.

If you're like most people, you probably have lots of questions about how to live a life that matters. You feel as though you have more to learn than can possibly be learned. But with smaller chunks of time and more sources of information than ever before, where can you turn for real insight and livable wisdom?

Barna Group has produced this series to examine the complicated issues of life and to help you live more meaningfully. We call it FRAMES—like a good set of eyeglasses that help you see the world more clearly ... or a work of art perfectly hung that invites you to look more closely ... or a building's skeleton, the part that is most essential to its structure.

The FRAMES Season 1 collection provides thoughtful and concise, data-driven and visually appealing insights for anyone who wants a more faith-driven and fulfilling life. In each FRAME we couple new cultural analysis from our team at Barna with an essay from leading voices in the field, providing information and ideas for you to digest in a more easily consumed number of words.

After all, it's a fast-paced world, full of words and images vying for your attention. Most of us have a number of half-read or "read someday" books on our shelves. But each FRAME aims to give you the essential information and real-life application behind one of today's most crucial trends in less than one-quarter the length of most books. These are big ideas in small books— designed so you truly can read less but know more. And the infographics and ideas in this FRAME are intended for share-ability. So read it, then find someone to "frame" with these ideas, and keep the conversation going (see "Share This Frame" on page 89).

Furthermore, each FRAME brings a distinctly Christian point of view to today's trends. In times of uncertainty, people look for guides. And we believe the Christian community is trying to make sense of the dramatic social changes happening around us.

Over the past thirty years, Barna Group has built a reputation as a trusted analyst of religion and culture. We offer cultural discernment for the Christian community by thoughtful analysts who care enough to tell the truth about what's really happening in today's society.

So sit back, but not for long. With FRAMES we invite you to read less and know more.

DAVID KINNAMAN
FRAMES, executive producer
president / Barna Group

ROXANNE STONE
FRAMES, general editor
vice president / Barna Group

Learn more at www.barnaframes.com.

F R A M E S

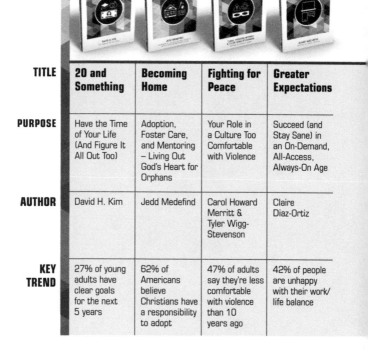

TITLE	20 and Something	Becoming Home	Fighting for Peace	Greater Expectations
PURPOSE	Have the Time of Your Life (And Figure It All Out Too)	Adoption, Foster Care, and Mentoring – Living Out God's Heart for Orphans	Your Role in a Culture Too Comfortable with Violence	Succeed (and Stay Sane) in an On-Demand, All-Access, Always-On Age
AUTHOR	David H. Kim	Jedd Medefind	Carol Howard Merritt & Tyler Wigg-Stevenson	Claire Diaz-Ortiz
KEY TREND	27% of young adults have clear goals for the next 5 years	62% of Americans believe Christians have a responsibility to adopt	47% of adults say they're less comfortable with violence than 10 years ago	42% of people are unhappy with their work/life balance

PERFECT FOR SMALL GROUP DISCUSSION

FRAMES Season 1: DVD
FRAMES Season 1: The Complete Collection

READ LESS.
KNOW MORE.

The Hyperlinked Life	Multi-Careering	Sacred Roots	Schools in Crisis	Wonder Women
Live with Wisdom in an Age of Information Overload	Do Work that Matters at Every Stage of Your Journey	Why Church Still Matters	They Need Your Help (Whether You Have Kids or Not)	Navigating the Challenges of Motherhood, Career, and Identity
Jun Young & David Kinnaman	Bob Goff	Jon Tyson	Nicole Baker Fulgham	Kate Harris
71% of adults admit they're overwhelmed by information	75% of adults are looking for ways to live a more meaningful life	51% of people don't think it's important to attend church	46% of Americans say public schools are worse than 5 years ago	72% of women say they're stressed

#BarnaFrames

www.barnaframes.com

Barna Group　　　ZONDERVAN®

BEFORE YOU READ

- What are the key factors you think make someone an adult? Financial independence? A degree? Marriage? An established career?

- If you're in your twenties, what are your top five goals to hit before you turn thirty?

- If you're older than thirty, what do you most regret not doing in your twenties?

- When you think about some of the defining moments of the last few decades (September 11, the global financial collapse, ongoing tension in the Middle East, the invention of the smartphone, the ushering in of social media), how do you think those events have shaped you?

- Many people are getting married later in life. Maybe you're one of them. Why do you think that is? What are the factors that have gone into delaying this life stage?

- When you think about your "dream job," what do you imagine? What are some key characteristics of that job?

- What do you think are some key differences between Millennials (adults age 18–29), Gen Xers (ages 30–48), and Boomers (ages 49–67)?

20 AND SOMETHING

Have the Time of Your Life (And Figure It All Out Too)

INFOGRAPHICS

THE ROARING 20s

Our culture loves youth, and many people would tell you the twenties "are the time of your life." So what makes this decade such a great one?

Top 5 things to do
BEFORE I TURN
30

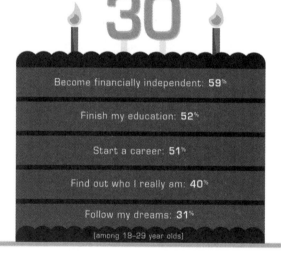

Become financially independent: **59**%

Finish my education: **52**%

Start a career: **51**%

Find out who I really am: **40**%

Follow my dreams: **31**%

(among 18-29 year olds)

TOP 5 THINGS I REGRET NOT DOING IN MY 20s
(among those over 30)

Finishing my education

Enjoying life more

Becoming more spiritually mature

Traveling to other countries

Finding out who I really am

What Makes an Adult?

When do you really truly become an adult? Once you've graduated from college? When you have your dream job? When you have a certain amount of financial stability? When you get married or have kids? Here are the factors respondents said define a grown-up.

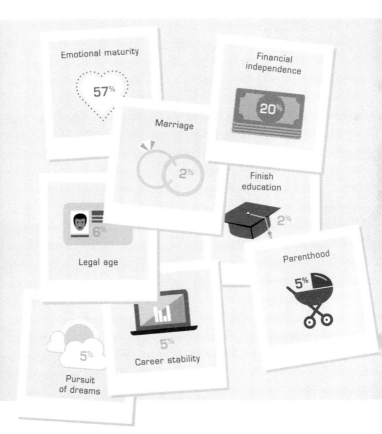

Emotional maturity
57%

Financial independence
20%

Marriage
2%

Finish education
2%

Legal age
6%

Parenthood
5%

Pursuit of dreams
5%

Career stability
5%

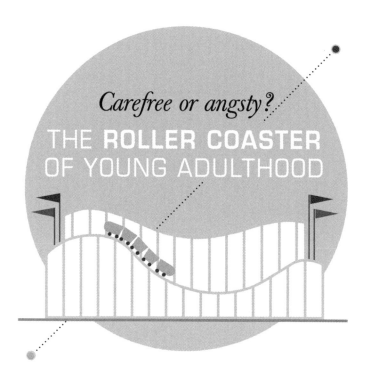

Carefree or angsty?

THE **ROLLER COASTER**
OF YOUNG ADULTHOOD

Your twenties can be quite the ride:
the highs of youth and optimism regularly
tempered by the lows of economic realities
and real-world problems. In so many ways,
it really is the best and worst of times.

Nearly 7 in 10 young adults are satisfied with life right now

Positive ·································▷

76% are very confident in their current life choices

62% like knowing more about tech than older adults

52% expect to have attained their dream job in 5 years

50% say their age is a benefit at work

33% know God is pleased with their priorities and choices

27% have clear goals for where they want to be in 5 years

◁······· Neutral ·······▷

33% worry they're disappointing those close to them

40% often feel lonely

45% feel judged by older adults for their life choices

48% aren't sure what God wants for their life

49% worry about choosing the wrong career

55% aren't sure if God is happy with their choices

◁································ Negative

20 AND SOMETHING

Have the Time of Your Life (And Figure It All Out Too)

FRAMEWORK

BY BARNA GROUP

The next greatest generation. The Me Me Me Generation. The generation some love to dump on. The list goes on — it seems everyone has something to say about twentysomethings.

But this group is not just *any* twentysomethings. Because this generation of Millennials is unique. The twentysomething life today is a different experience than it was for young adults of previous generations.

If you're in your twenties, you already sense this — and you're trying to navigate this life as it seems no one else has. After all, you're the only generation that's had to carefully monitor your social media while on the job hunt, knowing your Twitter page can be a make-or-break first impression. You're the first cohort of twentysomethings in which being married with a kid on the way makes you a minority among your peers. And you're the first generation to come of age in a truly global culture, thanks to a constant newsfeed of the latest innovations, entertainment, and current events.

Or maybe you're past your own twenties, but you care about the young adults in your life and are scratching your head as to what they really want and need in this transitional time. Or maybe you find yourself wondering why they seem to be so full of themselves when they rarely even get off the couch.

This book is for both you, the Millennial, and you, someone who wants to understand the twentysomethings in your life.

In the constant stream of interpretations about

Millennials, one thing is certain: Things are changing. Haven't you heard? "Thirty is the new twenty," or so they say, which reveals the fact that growing up as it has always before been defined has slowed down, even while everything else seems to have accelerated.

The tension stems from two different viewpoints about today's young adults. Are they a generation of narcissistic slackers? Or are they an echo of the Greatest Generation, destined to change the world for the good? Young or old, you likely have your own mixed feelings on the matter of generational differences and adulthood today.

If you're in your twenties, you're no doubt feeling the pressure to live up to the expectations of others' ideas for your life. The research for this FRAME tells us nearly half of all young adults feel judged by older adults for their life choices. More than two out of five say they sense pressure to grow up faster than they would like to. On the other hand, one-third believe older adults actually have lower expectations for them because of their fledgling adulthood.

But regardless of what anyone else thinks, twentysomethings are making their own way. So what does it look like today to be twenty and something?

Twenty and . . . Working?

If you're a twentysomething, you know exactly why older adults call you "the screwed generation." The recession hit you hard—as if you need yet another reminder. Not only that, but while you're working that entry-level job that's not in your field, you're carrying more debt than previous generations ever did at your age.

Nevertheless, our FRAMES research shows Millennials are serious about their work. In fact, 52% of young adults expect that in five years they will have their "dream job." Nearly the same percentage (49%) say they are anxious about choosing a career because they don't want to make the wrong choice.

Some may call it ambitious, some may call it unrealistic, but either way there is a sense of generational tension in the workplace. One out of every four twentysomethings say they feel held back by their age at work (24%) and about the same say they are not respected at work because of their age (23%).

Notably, these intangibles — such as respect — are often what Millennials value most in a job. The data show Millennials want passion for their job (42%), even more so than a job that helps them become financially secure (34%) or one that provides enough money to enjoy life (24%).

And while Millennials know they might not have as much career experience as their coworkers and superiors of older generations, there is one realm where they feel they are better qualified for the job: Nearly two-thirds of young adults say they "like that they know more" than older adults when it comes to technology. It's not empty confidence, either. When you consider the technological savvy and contributions digital natives have already offered in their short lifetimes, it's easy to see why they feel the way they do.

For these reasons and more, the twentysomething life today is a life of paradox. Tech savvy and ambitious, yet perceived by many as lazy and self-centered. Passionate and serious about work, yet job-hopping as they experiment and explore just where exactly to put that passion meaningfully to work.

As a Millennial, in many ways you have more opportunities and expectations than any generation before you. And yet, you can also anticipate a lot more headwinds in getting where you want to go.

Twenty and ... Married?

In the 1960s, twentysomethings were on the fast track to an established life. During that time in American social history, the vast majority of young adults were married, had kids, and lived outside their parents' home—all before the age of thirty. In fact, they were considered unconventional if they didn't. Single parenthood was a social anomaly. Opting for a career instead of a family was virtually unheard of—especially for women.

Today, this path looks drastically different. In fact, the majority of today's twentysomethings are anything but the formerly conventional married-plus-kids-plus-settled-on-a-lifetime-career trajectory. The Boomer generation completed most of those major life transitions before age thirty. But the Boomer generation wasn't growing up in the midst of the digitalization of culture.

Where family was the aspirational social structure of twentysomethings in previous generations, twentysomethings today are more interested in pursuing community through "digital tribes." They are exploring life not only with immediate friends and family, but with digitally connected groups of like-minded Millennials all over the world.

Marriage, children, career — these used to be the markers of adulthood. But not anymore. The definition of what makes someone an adult is undergoing change. Only 6% of adults today say adulthood is defined by legally coming of age. Only a few (2%) would say it's a result of marriage, and very few would say adulthood comes as a result of becoming a parent (5%) or having an established career (5%). In fact, regardless of generation, most adults (57%) agree the true marker of becoming a "grown-up" is emotional maturity.

So if they're moving away from marriage and family as driving goals in their twenties, what *do* Millennials really want? Among eighteen- to twenty-nine-year-olds, the most important goals they want to achieve before reaching age thirty include becoming financially independent from their moms and dads (59%), finishing their education (52%) and starting a career (51%). After that, they hope to find out who they really are (40%), follow their dreams (31%), and become more spiritually mature (29%).

MARRIAGE FOR MILLENNIALS

While the vast majority of unmarried young adults want to be married at some point, it's not a priority right now for most of them. And, in fact, they'd like to get a lot of things in order first.

82% *"I want to be married at some point"*

BUT FIRST ...

70%
I want to be fully developed as a person

69%
I want to be financially established

60%
I think we should live together

3/10 Unmarried Millennials say they aren't sure if they believe in the conventional form of marriage

This leaves getting married the seventh most important objective among today's young adults (28%), which is only slightly higher than enjoying life before you have the responsibilities of adulthood (24%). Parenthood is a goal by age thirty among just one-fifth of today's Millennials (21%). This is equaled by the percent of Millennials who say they aspire to travel overseas before they reach their thirtieth birthday.

But—and here there needs to be a but—this doesn't mean Millennials don't want to be married and have kids. Rather, the Millennial attitude toward marriage and kids can be summed up in one word: someday. And in the meantime, they're trying to build toward it. The vast majority (82%) want to get married someday, but they believe you should be financially established (69%) and "fully developed as a person" (70%) before you say your vows. And 60% believe "it's a good idea to live with a person before you get married," perhaps as more evidence of this generation's experimental tendencies driven by the desire to make the right choice.

Again, despite the perceptions that twentysomethings are self-centered, unmotivated, and lazy, the FRAMES data show they're serious about planning well for their future. In fact, their worst fear is perhaps being under-prepared. The number of young adults today who feel equipped to be married are in the minority—only 40%. Even less (36%) say they feel ready to have kids.

Twentysomethings may appear, to some, as prolonging their adolescence. Yet in many ways, this generation is waiting for the perfect moment to dive in.

Twenty and . . . Faithful?

So what does all this in-between living look like when it comes to church? The trend is not promising, according to our surveys. Today's eighteen- to twenty-nine-year-olds are the least likely of all age groups to believe churches have their best interests at heart. And while there are millions of churchgoing twentysomethings in the US and elsewhere, most young adults who grow up as Christians (59%) end up leaving the church at some point after high school graduation.

Many pastors dismiss this exodus by saying, "We don't need to worry about young church dropouts because everyone knows they'll come back when they get married and have kids."

Yet this raises an unsettling question: Why can so many people accept the fact Boomers put their unique stamp on society but then minimize the uniqueness of Millennials? Just as the sexual revolution of the 1960s continues to echo, the rise of digital tribes of twentysomethings is profoundly influencing the spiritual trajectory of this emerging generation. And it's too important for us to miss.

Despite mixed feelings about church and organized religion, young adults have not given up on deeper questions. The FRAMES research shows one of the most significant ambitions of today's young adults is to find a life of "meaning." An overwhelming 87% of today's Millennials want to live a meaningful life.

Here, of course, the church has something to give.

But first it is going to have to learn how to genuinely connect the dots — from vocation to prayer life to Instagram feed — for a life of meaning. Our research shows just how important this holistic integration of faith is. Among churchgoing Millennials, 45% have learned to understand their gifts and passions as part of God's calling, while 83% of church dropouts say the church has not helped them to learn this.

Many young adults are finding deep connection in churches. Yet what Millennials are after, above all, is a life of meaning. And if the church isn't offering this, Millennials will go elsewhere to find it.

Twenty and ... Something?

David Kim, a pastor at Redeemer Church in New York City, has been connecting these dots — between faith, work, family, friendships — among twentysomethings for years. And in this FRAME, he will dig deeper into the reasons this generation is unlike any before it and what they need to thrive in the midst of transition.

Then in the Re/Frame, demonstrating the potency of intergenerational wisdom, we invite you to listen in on publishing entrepreneur Phyllis Tickle. She offers wisdom — some of it new and some of it very old — for living faithfully and well in this often tumultuous decade of life.

As you read this FRAME, try to put your stereotypes about young and old on pause. If you're inclined toward optimism or pessimism toward Millennials, please suspend your gut instinct. Instead, discern in these pages something deeper, more akin to the biblical ideals of faith, hope, and love — ideals that, young or young at heart, will help us enjoy life and figure it all out too. ◆

20 AND SOMETHING

Have the Time of Your Life (And Figure It All Out Too)

THE FRAME

BY DAVID H. KIM

Why would you turn down a job offer from Google?! You are going to work where? For how much? But ... why?

This was Stephanie's parents' response when she told them she'd given up a coveted opportunity at the "number one company to work for" (according to *Fortune* magazine) to instead work at a small nonprofit for barely more than minimum wage.

For many, the mere idea of turning down job security, a great salary, and the opportunity to work for an industry-leading company with a world-changing mission would be incomprehensible. But after weeks of careful deliberation, recent college graduate Stephanie did just that. Despite her parents' best efforts to convince her otherwise, she stuck to her convictions and spent the next few years serving this small nonprofit for which she felt a strong personal connection.

Perhaps you know someone like Stephanie — someone who has given up a lucrative career to instead work for a start-up nonprofit with a compelling mission. Or maybe you know someone like Justin who does illustration and contract design work for a number of well-known organizations — all from his living room with his one-year-old nearby. Or you might have a friend like Andia, who is putting together a fashion show and local design showcase after a successful Kickstarter campaign. Or Chris, a videographer/musician/small business owner who could never imagine doing just one thing.

Entrepreneurs. Freelancers. Idealists.

Maybe you are one.

What do Stephanie, Justin, Andia, and Chris have in common? They are twentysomethings in this second decade of the twenty-first century. In other words, nothing and everything. They live in different parts of the country, and they are from different racial and economic backgrounds. They have different levels of education and different dreams for the future. But each of them is navigating a decade of life that just doesn't look like it used to.

Coming of Age in a Changing World

Having worked closely with people in their twenties for almost two decades now, I can safely say this: The times, they're changing! In fact, that is about the most certain thing I can say regarding this formative decade of life and this generation that has entered into it. While no generation likes to be stereotyped or pigeonholed, trying to label this generation is like putting tape on water—nothing really seems to stick—except, perhaps, change. They are a generation eager to advance real change.

And why shouldn't they be? Twentysomethings today came of age during some of the most significant changes our world has ever seen: the development of the Internet, a new magnitude of global and local terrorism, a devastating financial collapse, and scandals at the highest levels of trusted institutions.

These are just a few of the culture-shaping events that have formed twentysomethings and the world they must now inhabit. And yet, despite good reasons for the contrary, at the heart of this generation is an undaunted sense of hope. Even after having witnessed the past hopes of society falter, twentysomethings continue to hope, which drives them toward change. This drive is not one with a singularity of focus, but one that meanders and allows its passengers to take time for fun along the way. And why not? They're in their twenties, after all.

Millennials: Who Are They?

As I write this, the current Millennials were born from 1984 to 1993. And although technically the twentysomethings are a subset of the Millennials, for this book I will be using Millennials and twentysomethings interchangeably.

Millennials are, to borrow from Winston Churchill, "a riddle wrapped in a mystery inside an enigma" — especially to older generations. They can be a confusing group when you look at their decisions and their outlook on life. Perhaps that's why each week there is a lengthening list of articles published about them — many of them by Millennials about Millennials for those who aren't Millennials. This generation of young adults has come of age and is now trying to make sense of life — to find work, meaning, and love — while the rest of the world attempts to make sense of them.

Despite these many attempts to understand the members of this generation, they respond in ways that defy simple characterization. Certainly, common factors have shaped and influenced what has been dubbed the "Me Me Me Generation." These external factors have not created a particular mold for twentysomethings but rather an incubator of countless creative possibilities. When you follow the steady stream of articles and books written on this group of eighty million young adults, you might find yourself more confused by the apparent contradictions you read. Who are the Millennials, really? Are they the entitled, narcissistic, Internet addicts who are the "Worst. Generation. Ever?" Or the entrepreneurial, socially conscious geniuses who will undo all the problems previous generations have left behind?

The answer to that question is as complicated as the converging factors that are influencing this generation's coming of age—factors that each pose unique challenges.

Technology

This is the first generation to have access to the world from the day they learned how to use a computer, and the Internet developed alongside the maturing Millennials. Today the impact and global reach one Millennial can have is unprecedented. For example, consider the staggering number of Twitter followers today's Millennial pop stars have: Lady Gaga, more than 40 million followers; Katy Perry, more than 42.6 million followers; and to top it off, Justin Bieber has more than 44.4 million followers, with that number growing each day. Each of these pop icons has more people attuned to their tweets than live in the top twenty-five US cities combined. It is hard to overstate the impact Internet-based technologies, like social media, have had and will have upon the world, and twentysomethings have been on the pioneering edge of this digital revolution.

Terrorism

I will always remember the day of the Virginia Tech University shootings. I was in the student center at Princeton University watching the breaking news of this massacre on the big-screen television. About thirty students were intently watching the incredulous scene unfold. During one of the commercial breaks, I looked around and was astonished by the dozens of other students going about their normal business of studying, playing pool, and talking on their cell phones. Despite the tragedy on another college campus, these students seemed unfazed or undisturbed by what was going on. It was almost as if this shooting was not all that unique, and perhaps for them, it wasn't.

These were the students, after all, who had watched with the nation as four hijacked planes targeted some of America's most iconic buildings in an unimaginable act of terrorism. During the years to follow, that sense of safety and trust that previous generations took for granted had been irreversibly changed as evidenced by the unprecedented rise in security from airports to elementary schools. As teenagers, Millennials were growing up in a post 9/11 world, witnessing school shootings from Columbine (high school) to Virginia Tech and, more recently, Sandy Hook (elementary school).

Terror could strike not only in the halls of power but also in the most unsuspecting places, like a movie theater in Aurora, Colorado, or the final yards of the Boston Marathon, making the world seem even more dangerous, capricious, and senseless. Millennials experienced the reality of terrorism from abroad and from within in ways no previous American generation witnessed—and all of it in looped HD.

Institutions

Many of the institutions previous generations respected as the pillars of a healthy society became disgraced by scandals during the Millennials' formative years. Corruption was exposed within trusted institutions like government, big corporations, national sports teams, and organized religion. In the political arena, the 1998 Clinton-Lewinsky sex scandal demonstrated that infidelity and a breach in integrity were quite possible even in the highest political office in our country. President Clinton may have eventually been acquitted by the Senate of his impeachment charges of perjury and obstruction of justice, but this trial placed the moral failure of America's highest elected official at the center of national media.

Then in October 2001, the Enron Corporation was

embroiled in a scandal that involved the deliberate mismanagement of billions of dollars, which led to what was at that time the largest corporate bankruptcy in American history. The Enron scandal also resulted in the discrediting of one of the world's largest audit companies, Arthur Anderson. Shortly after, another major corporation, WorldCom, filed for Chapter 11 bankruptcy due to accounting scandals that inflated the company's assets by approximately $11 billion.

And in the arena of religion, in early 2002 the *Boston Globe* exposed a series of sexual abuse scandals in the Catholic diocese of Boston, one of the largest Catholic dioceses in America. The *Globe* revealed the Catholic Church had been aware of patterns of sexual abuse and chose to cover up these incidents. This exposé began a frenzy of media investigations that continues to this day, with accusations in the thousands. And the Millennials' sports heroes toppled too: from Lance Armstrong's stripped titles because of using performance-enhancing drugs, to Tiger Woods' infidelities, to the massive sexual abuse cover-ups at Penn State. The message seemed clear: There's no one you can really trust; everyone has a secret. Even Martha Stewart ended up in prison.

Recession

Then in 2008 another key corporation, Lehman Brothers, American's fourth largest investment bank, declared bankruptcy, contributing to what would become a global recession in 2009. Lehman's bankruptcy was part of a much larger financial

THE INSTITUTION AND ME

Millennials trust institutions more than older generations do …
except for church. Though their trust for church is relatively higher,
they trust it less than older generations.

"I believe they have my best interests at heart"

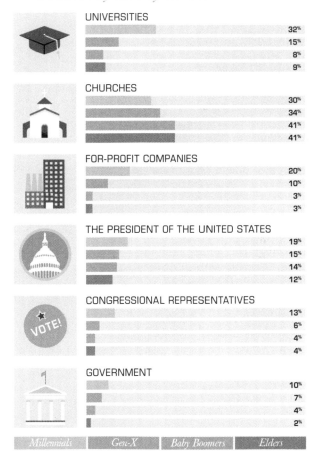

UNIVERSITIES
- 32%
- 15%
- 8%
- 9%

CHURCHES
- 30%
- 34%
- 41%
- 41%

FOR-PROFIT COMPANIES
- 20%
- 10%
- 3%
- 3%

THE PRESIDENT OF THE UNITED STATES
- 19%
- 15%
- 14%
- 12%

CONGRESSIONAL REPRESENTATIVES
- 13%
- 6%
- 4%
- 4%

GOVERNMENT
- 10%
- 7%
- 4%
- 2%

Millennials   *Gen-X*   *Baby Boomers*   *Elders*

meltdown, including the sub-prime mortgage crisis. And in the years following, unemployment levels have climbed and prospects for economic growth throughout the country remain limited. Many of the Millennials now graduating from college with high hopes and huge debts are experiencing the unanticipated difficulty of finding gainful employment. Suddenly everyone is wondering if this will be the first American generation since the Great Depression to be worse off financially than their parents.

Of course narcissism and optimism, rebellion and hope are almost always present in twentysomethings of every generation. They are a special combination that contributes to what has always been a formative life stage. Today's twentysomethings are not so different from their predecessors in that way. And yet, it would be a mistake to leave it at that. The changes and volatility of the last two decades in American history have shaped the particular response of this generation in some specific ways. They have encountered a world quite different from that of previous generations and have responded to these challenging circumstances with an unexpected amount of hope and ambition for the future. And it is through that lens Millennials are viewing some of the age-old questions countless generations before them have sought answers to in their youth: What is the meaning of life? What do I do with my life? And, of course, what is love — aka, with whom do I spend the rest of my life?

What Is the Meaning of Life?

YOLO.

If you don't know what it means, you're probably not a Millennial. It's texting shorthand for "you only live once." What was *carpe diem* for one generation is now YOLO for another, and these four letters capture well this generation's sentiment of wanting to make the most of this one life they've got.

About eight years ago, this phrase hadn't yet been coined, but it was still informing the Millennial experience. My friend Jared had just finished his first year in business school and was gearing up to lead an expedition team to Antarctica. Who would have imagined a generation ago that a twentysomething would be leading an expedition to this remote and frigid part of the world? Business schools have done their market research. They know not only what can develop leadership skills but also what will appeal to this generation of leaders. If you want to attract top talent, you do it with the lure of these once-in-a-lifetime experiences. Yet there's a larger context that informs and shapes this generation's desire for unique adventure.

Sure, YOLO is a tongue-in-cheek catchphrase. But it says something about the sincere quest for meaning many Millennials are after. It also speaks to two other values in the twentysomething imagination — hope and change.

These two words are certainly not unique to this generation like YOLO is, but it was no coincidence

Obama's slogans were "Hope" and "Change" in 2008 and "Forward" in 2012. In both elections, Millennial support was crucial for his victory. Obama's campaign managers, as well as those who know Millennials, keenly understand that what brings meaning to this generation is hope leading to change. The truly inspiring stories seemed to emerge from unexpected people and places: college dropouts like Steve Jobs and Bill Gates, start-up nonprofits like Kiva, charity: water, and Teach For America. These stories reinforced the Millennial ideal: A broken world doesn't have to stay broken. So why not try to change the world or at least some part of it? After all, YOLO. But where, exactly, this generation will choose to channel its hope for change is another question. And we can rule out several channels right away.

Where They Aren't Finding Meaning

Politics

It could easily be argued that President Obama understands this generation unlike any other presidential candidate. He deftly employed the rhetoric they wanted to hear and expertly used technology and art to inspire Millennials. Yet by early 2010, their support for Obama waned, in part because the change they sought never quite materialized. Despite the surge in political interest, Millennials' initial hopes for political change turned into cynicism toward public officials. In our FRAMES research, two in three Millennials admit most people they vote for end up disappointing them. Only 10% believe the government

has their best interests at heart, and slightly more (13%) would say their congressional representatives do. President Obama gains slightly more of their trust, with 19% believing "the president has my best interests at heart." However, whether or not they believe he has their best interests at heart, Millennials aren't convinced he can actually do anything about it: 65% of Millennials say no single politician can make a positive difference, and nearly seven in ten (68%) believe the government will never actually change for the better.

With such a bleak perspective, it's no wonder less than half of Millennials (48%) consider themselves politically active. While Millennials still want to believe their participation matters — two-thirds say they could make a

THE POLITICAL DIVIDE

Millennials are notoriously bad at showing up to vote. Why? Here are a few clues:

Most people I vote for end up disappointing me:

☑ **YES** 65%   ☐ **NO** 35%

Government will never change for the better:

☑ **YES** 68%   ☐ **NO** 32%

A single politician can make a difference:

☐ **YES** 35%   ☑ **NO** 65%

I can make a difference if I'm politically active.

☑ **YES** 64%   ☐ **NO** 36%

I consider myself to be politically active:

☐ **YES** 48%   ☑ **NO** 52%

THAT'S BAD BUSINESS

They may be the most marketed-to generation in history, but Millennials remain skeptical of and believe the following about big business:

61%
are too focused on profits

52%
pay their executives too much

48%
aren't loyal to their workers

46%
pay low wages

36%
don't care about the environment

difference if they were politically active — their low voter turnout during recent off-year and special elections would seem to offer proof of a growing disillusionment.

Large Corporations

The confidence of Millennials fares even worse when it comes to big corporations, which are increasingly global. With scandals such as Enron's and WorldCom's, as well as Main Street's growing negativity toward Wall Street during the financial crisis, Millennials saw the corruptive tendencies endemic in big business. Opaque and fiscally unethical business practices led to a loss in confidence that big corporations could actually change the world for the better. Millennials watched as banks failed, the housing market collapsed, and historic sectors such as the auto industry scrambled to stay alive. Even beloved companies like Gap and Apple had their overseas working conditions questioned.

Again and again, Millennials saw corporations choose greed and power over social good. Perhaps all that marketing exposure at a young age did work, though, as Millennials are more optimistic about the role of corporations in society than other generations— Millennials are twice as likely as Gen Xers and nearly seven times as likely as Boomers or Elders to trust for-profit corporations. Even so, they are deeply troubled by what they've witnessed in corporate America. Millennials identify a number of problems with big business, including an inordinate focus on profits (61%), extravagant executive pay (52%), disloyalty toward workers (48%), inadequate wages for workers (46%), a disregard for the environment (36%), and an unfair tax advantage (25%).

Higher Education

Even hallowed institutions like higher education have come under suspicion as a conduit for meaning. Like many previous generations, Millennials grew up being told pursuing higher education would lead to greater career opportunities and economic mobility. A college education and advanced degrees were seen as key steps toward realizing the American dream, and in following this trusted wisdom, Millennials are expected to become the most educated generation in history.[1] Yet, as any young adult today saddled with school loans knows, such an esteemed superlative does not come without a catch.

In fact, the traditional commencement speech platitudes welcoming students into the vast opportunities of adulthood — "the whole world is before you"; you just have to "follow your dreams" to "make a true difference" — often ring hollow in this depressed economy. Hundreds of thousands of graduating Millennials are discovering the world is not their oyster, and jobs are much harder to find than anyone had expected. Two-thirds of the class of 2010 had student loans averaging approximately $25,000.[2] Unfortunately, many Millennials may have mortgaged their future to pursue an education that won't pay off financially. In 2012, Millennials' unemployment rates had risen to 37%, up 7% from 2007.[3] And only half of under-twenty-five college graduates who are working are working at a job that requires a college degree.[4]

Of course, as a Millennial, you don't need statistics to tell you student loans are burdensome and job prospects are dwindling — this is your daily experience. Even as you hope and hold out for the "perfect job," it's easy to despair that there will ever be a job. And as such it's easy to question the value of higher education and what it's *really* giving you in the long run. Only four in ten college graduates would say they need their degree for their current job (42%) or that it's related to the work they're doing (40%), and the same number wish they'd chosen a different major altogether. In the end, just under half of Millennials (47%) would strongly agree their degree was worth the cost and time. And it's no wonder this number has dropped below half, especially when online courses and MOOCs (massive open online courses) from preeminent universities are being posted

WORTH THE PAPER IT'S PRINTED ON

Many young adults today are graduating from college
with a lot of debt and not a lot of job prospects.
So was getting that degree worth the cost and time?

College prepared me for life: **36**%

\+

I need my degree for my job: **42**%

\+

My degree is related to my current job: **40**%

\−

I wish I'd picked a different major: **40**%

\−

I should have gone to a different college: **29**%

Worth it:
47%

on the Internet for free. Especially when you've got a political science degree but can't seem to get a job that doesn't involve a green smock and an espresso machine.

Even so, this degree-to-job disparity seems to be bothering parents most of all. While only about one-third of Millennials believe universities "have my best interests at heart," that is nearly twice as many as Gen Xers (15%) and four times as many as Boomers (8%). Considering most Millennials remain optimistic about someday achieving that "dream job" (52% believe it's within reach in the next five years), it would seem they still believe the degree will pay off at some point.

Church

With all this scandal and disillusionment swirling around them, one might expect this generation would look to religion to find inspiration. Isn't this what previous generations have always done — found meaning and purpose in organized religion? Haven't churches throughout American history functioned as a force for hope and change?

But Millennials don't see it that way. They are a generation that has developed heightened radar for institutional corruption. And they see the church as another fallible institution.

In fact, while Millennials are more trusting in general of institutions than older generations, church is the one exception. In our FRAMES research, Millennials were the least likely generation to say the church has their best interests at heart. This is a reality reflected by a decline in church attendance—less than half have attended church in the last six months, and even among young adults who grew up going to church, six in ten have dropped out at some point.

In fact, today approximately 25% of Millennials decline to affiliate with any organized religion.[5] However, such apparent religious apathy does not mean this generation is devoid of faith. Many Millennials still consider themselves to be spiritual, and in fact, Millennials are about as likely to pray as prior generations at their age.[6] Twentysomethings may be leaving the church, but they aren't leaving faith.

Millennials do not find their values reflected within the church. Twentysomethings prize authenticity, cohesiveness, and tolerance, but perceive Christianity to be intolerant and exclusive, culturally irrelevant and hostile to those living nontraditional lifestyles, at least from an evangelical perspective. They also came of age just as many prominent Christian leaders were exposed to be living hypocritical lives. The abuse scandals among Roman Catholic priests and the moral downfall of well-known Protestant megachurch pastors have received an abundance of media attention and driven many young adults to question why they should turn to the church as a moral authority.

And that's just in the national spotlight. For many, church disillusionment is a profoundly personal experience: a church split, an admired pastor or mentor not being who you thought they were, or just far too many friends being burned by church experiences.

It's easy to wonder, why take the risk? Moreover, why go to church when you can download much better sermons by a pastor from a faraway church and listen to them as you run on your treadmill?

Churches, of course, are realizing this. Yet it seems their efforts to reach Millennials are often falling flat. The truth is that many young adults today aren't looking for a hipper coffee bar, more contemporary worship, or better cultural references in sermons. Simply put, they're looking for depth — spiritual relevance that connects to the world they live in.

Millennials yearn for an experience that includes and makes sense of their whole world and have a strong distaste for an "us" versus "them" mentality. They see a world around them they want to actively engage, not run away from. This generation wants a faith that is authentic, charitable, and embracing, and many just don't see that in the church.

Millennials are going to turn to whatever helps them in their search for meaning. Right now, that's often family and personal interests — which they would rank as most central to their identity. But it could be the church again. I know, because I'm seeing it happen.

Six years ago, I took a job in New York City — one of the most unchurched cities in America and an epicenter for twentysomethings. I was hired to create curriculum for a nine-month leadership development program for Millennials. The goals of this program were threefold — theological, spiritual, and community formation and integration. It was an ambitious, if not risky, endeavor

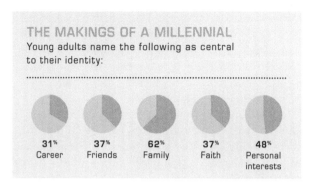

THE MAKINGS OF A MILLENNIAL
Young adults name the following as central
to their identity:

| **31%** | **37%** | **62%** | **37%** | **48%** |
| Career | Friends | Family | Faith | Personal interests |

for an urban church. First, because the program itself wasn't cheap — $2,200 per participant. Second, there was a significant time investment. Participants would have to commit to meeting two hours each week, one full Saturday every month, with three retreats scattered throughout the year. In addition, there were significant weekly reading and project requirements.

In a city with limitless ways to fill your calendar, would busy, commitment-averse New Yorkers actually be interested in a program like this?

In these six years, we have been surprised and delighted to find the answer to that question has been yes. Every year, the number of applications increases, and we now have to turn away more than 50% of applicants for our limited forty-two spots. Among all our participants over the years, we've discovered a deep hunger for spiritual, theological, and relational integration and transformation. Millennials want a faith and spirituality that is real and connects to the complex public realities they face each day. They want their faith to be a holistic part of their work lives, beyond the opportunity for workplace evangelism. They want to know how to live out their faith in the gray areas. And they want to know what it means to be a Christian not only on Sundays but throughout the week.

Millennials don't necessarily want to leave the faith, but there is dwindling patience for the church's segregation of secular and sacred. Twentysomethings want to change themselves *and* the world. And when they do leave the church, it's often because they are finding more hope for real change outside of it.

Just ask Christine. She was working with a tech company, dreaming with her coworkers about how they could change the world. Christine loved going to work because it was a place where she could think big. But then on Sundays, she'd go to church, and unlike her coworkers, people there seemed to her to be more concerned about keeping themselves separate from the world than creating something of substance within it.

Christine was caught up in a grand vision at work, with the exciting prospects of changing the industry and even life as we know it. But at church, despite the message of a world-changing gospel, there seemed to be very little interest in actually living out that message. In Christine's eyes, there was only a subculture — and she wasn't sure she wanted to be part of it anymore.

In the not-so-distant past, institutions were trusted as important agents of societal change. After all, that's what they were for — government, corporations, higher education, organized religion. This generation doesn't look at institutions in the same way. What is striking, however, is that the widespread corruption, scandal, and crisis haven't stopped Millennials from hoping. Sure, it has stopped them from trusting these societal institutions to follow through on the change they promise, but Millennials *are* still hoping for change. They've just transferred that hope from institutions to individuals, to small organizations, to start-ups, to grassroots movements. And that, they believe, is where they'll find meaning.

When it comes to the pursuit of meaning, Millennials have discovered that sometimes the best way to change the world is to shoulder that change yourself. And why not? We've seen it happen many times before. We've watched as college dropouts and fresh graduates become multi-billionaires. From pioneering social media companies like Facebook to online fundraisers like KickStarter to the grassroots media-driven activism like Invisible Children, twentysomethings are already changing the world as we know it.

Remember Stephanie and her two job offers? She took the less obvious path. As prestigious as a job offer from Google was, in her mind Google would always be there. On the other hand, working for the nonprofit gave her an opportunity to make a concrete change in the lives of people she had come to know and love.

Surprising? Maybe. But then again, that's the Millennial style.

In the middle of your twenties, navigating new jobs,

lease agreements, and student loans, it can be difficult to envision what life will look like in five to ten years. But what may appear to the outside world to be a meandering road is actually a journey of meaning — meaning that is found in the hope of changing this world for the better and having some fun while you're at it.

Because, after all, you *do* only live once.

What Do I Do with My Life?

In 2011, comedian Conan O'Brien delivered a commencement speech to the graduating class at Dartmouth University, complete with requisite hyperbole and sarcasm but containing an uncomfortable truth nonetheless. "Today," he began, "you have achieved something special — something only 92% of Americans your age will ever know: a college diploma. That's right, with your college diploma you now have a crushing advantage over 8% of the workforce. I'm talking about dropout losers like Bill Gates, Steve Jobs, and Mark Zuckerberg."

He then went on to address the parents of this esteemed crowd with the following advice: "Many of you haven't seen your children in four years. Now you are about to see them every day when they come out of the basement to tell you the Wi-Fi isn't working ... You will spend more money framing your child's diploma than they will earn in the next six months. It's tough out there, so be patient. The only people hiring right now are Panera

Bread and Mexican drug cartels. Yes, you parents must be patient because it is indeed a grim job market out there. And one of the reasons it's so tough finding work is that aging Baby Boomers refuse to leave their jobs."[7]

In today's depressed economy, it seems fitting to have a comedian give the final words to a graduating class because you can either laugh or cry at the truth of our economic situation. But for many, our times are anything but humorous. Having graduated from high school and college, Millennials are facing the reality of scarce jobs and low wages. In the midst of the Occupy Wall Street movement, the media began spinning stories of mobs of restless, disenchanted, and unemployed young adults whipped into a frustrated frenzy and storming corporate America.

But the truth about the Occupy Wall Street movement is that it fizzled very quickly, arguably because it failed to broadly inspire the Millennials, who are driven by hopeful pragmatism more than stagnant protest. And in the end, the Occupy Wall Street movement *wasn't* a movement; it was a stand-in-place demand for change. But Millennials, if nothing else, are a generation that insists on movement.

Here's the reality of what is broken: The current economic climate poses great challenges for job-hunting twentysomethings. The employment rate of eighteen- to thirty-one-year-olds in 2012 was 63%.[8] Even those young adults who are college educated are struggling to find employment, with the rate of unemployment of twentysomethings holding a BA degree or higher jumping from 7.7% in 2007 to 13.3% in 2012.[9] Given

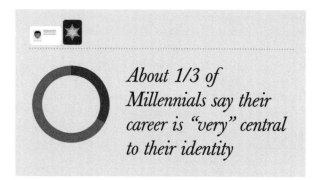

About 1/3 of Millennials say their career is "very" central to their identity

these statistics, it would be easy in this depressed job market for Millennials to become extremely nervous about their financial situations and cynical about work.

Yet, despite the bleak economic landscape, Millennials remain optimistic about their future prospects. As mentioned earlier, more than half of Millennials surveyed for our FRAMES research believe they will have attained their dream job within the next five years. Nearly nine in ten Millennials (88%) believe they currently have enough money or will eventually meet their long-term financial goals.[10] Even among the unemployed and financially strapped, 75% of Millennials indicate they will someday have enough money. They are more optimistic about their economic future than older generations. While 55% of Americans over fifty-five believe young people will have a worse life than their parents, less than half of Millennials agree.

Two years ago, James, a Millennial who worked in the banking industry, was laid off like so many of his colleagues. He didn't want to waste any time in "funemployment," so he immediately went on the job hunt, actively checking in with headhunters and friends. As his search continued, James thought long and hard about the kind of work he wanted to do. This unemployment was an opportunity to rethink his career goals. He realized he no longer wanted a banking job, but to be in the entrepreneurial sector, so he narrowed his search even further.

Weeks turned into months, and he was nearing a year of living off of his savings. What might be surprising to hear was that during this time he had at least three job offers from reputable financial firms; however, they were not in his specified area of interest, so he turned them down. In these difficult economic times, one might counsel James to just take a job that pays the bills. Not the Millennials. Not even a year of unemployment could dampen the hope of finding the right job, and for James it paid off (this time). Fifteen months after being laid off, James found his dream job in venture capital.

One of the reasons Millennials are so resilient in the face of a tough job environment is that many of them refuse to be defined and confined by their job choices or lack thereof. In fact, only 31% would say career is central to their identity—listing it lower than any other factor except technology. Millennials see their twenties as a time to explore their career options so they can find a job that will provide that sense of meaning and fulfillment. This may be a little confounding to their parents. Two-thirds of Boomers would say "starting your career" is crucial in your twenties, while only half of Millennials would agree. When it comes to work and career, more than anything this generation of Millennials wants to be inspired. Finding a job they are passionate about is the career priority Millennials ranked highest (42%). They don't want a job merely for the sake of a paycheck, and they are willing to wait to find the right job. Some may interpret this willingness to wait as a sign of courage, while others may view it as colossal irresponsibility. Having grown up in an era where parents and teachers were constantly telling them they could "be whatever you want to be," many Millennials see this decision as their prerogative, even if it means having to live off unemployment benefits or parental assistance.

Because job satisfaction and fulfillment are so important to this generation, Millennials refuse to compromise on what they want out of work, which is a lot: They cite working for themselves, a job adaptable to their strengths, having a lot of variety, and the freedom to take risks as essential career priorities, in addition to being able to fund their personal interests. The Millennial perspective on work has baffled many, and numerous companies have hired consultants to better understand and adapt to this new generation of workers.

Millennials have overwhelmingly indicated that working in a positive work environment where their input is valued is extremely important to them, suggesting Millennials prefer to work in organizations where the structure is "flatter" and less hierarchical.[11] Millennials want regular feedback and expect to be praised when they do a good job. They also want to work in a stimulating atmosphere, where they can release their creative passions. For many who are older, these characteristics and expectations make the Millennials a challenge to work with.

In terms of social impact, twentysomethings have demonstrated a strong desire to work at a job that has a positive impact on causes and issues that are important to them.[12] A recent poll of college students showed the number-one desired place of employment was St. Jude's Children's Hospital, supplanting tech giant Google.[13] They feel corporate employers should be socially conscious and have a "triple bottom line" — being conscious of their profits, their impact on the environment, and their treatment of workers. Nearly two-thirds of Millennials surveyed indicated the biggest

THIS IS MY "DREAM JOB"

More than half of young adults believe they'll have it in five years, but what exactly do Millennials think of when they imagine that dream job?

24%
42%
34%

- I feel passionate about it
- It offers me financial security
- It gives me enough money to enjoy life

49% of Millennials are anxious about making the wrong career choice problem with corporations today is that they focus too much on profits.

This elevation of job fulfillment over security has led to an increase in job-hopping among young adults. Statistics show Millennials just assume they will have multiple career changes. Gone are the days when an entry-level employee could expect to remain with one employer throughout his or her career. While the average worker today remains at his or her job for 4.4 years, Millennials generally expect to remain at a job for less than three years.[14]

One consequence of all this job-hopping, which we'll look at in more detail later, is the delay of starting a family. Millennials are getting married later in life because they're finding that "stable job" much later in life than previous generations. Twentysomethings also don't want to be encumbered by the responsibilities inherent in family life so they can have the freedom to take on jobs that might not be able to pay all the bills that come with a family.

Millennials seem to find many ways to turn proverbial lemons into lemonade, maintaining a positive outlook on their bleak job prospects by turning to a less conventional solution: entrepreneurship. In a recent *New York Times* article, William Deresiewicz opined on what he dubbed "Generation Sell."[15] Deresiewicz maintained, "Today's ideal social form is not the commune or the movement or even the individual creator as such; it's the small business. Every artistic or moral aspiration — music, food, good works, what have you — is expressed in those terms."[16] He attributed the ubiquitous nature of this entrepreneurial spirit to the dot.com era and to a distrust of large organizations. He notes that today's hero is the entrepreneur and cites the late Steve Jobs as "our new deity."[17]

Technological advances have played an important role in nurturing the entrepreneurial mind-set of this twentysomething generation. It has never been easier for a would-be entrepreneur to access information and obtain funding for budding projects. Crowd-sourcing sites like Kickstarter and Indiegogo have helped to cultivate an entrepreneurial culture among young adults around the world.

In fact, a survey commissioned by oDesk and Millennial Branding found that 58% of Millennials would call themselves entrepreneurial.[18] In embracing an entrepreneurial mind-set, twentysomethings have used this route as a vehicle for their creativity and independence. Among those surveyed, 38% responded that they would rather join a promising start-up than complete a college degree.[19] Success stories like Google and Facebook serve as inspirational fodder for twentysomethings who are hungry for success as they would define it. For Millennials, the entrepreneurial lifestyle celebrates everything they have come to want in their work lives: self-drive, creativity, and an opportunity to use their jobs to make an impact on issues and causes they care about. In our FRAMES research, Millennials prioritize working for themselves as an important career priority more than any other generation. These young adults want to make their own hours, come to work in their jeans and flip-flops, and save the world while they're at it.

Even those who have gainful employment often view their full-time jobs as simply a "day job," and in their spare time they focus on entrepreneurial passions and interests. I know a small group of Millennials who all have hectic full-time jobs, and during their spare hours they are creating a new social media app that facilitates real-life interaction. They believe life should be lived with people in community, and instead of marginalizing technology to achieve that, they are using it to encourage face-to-face interactions. As if one full-time job weren't enough, when prompted by a vision, these young adults are willing to work hard to see their vision materialize.

Even the risk associated with entrepreneurialism is a value for Millennials, nearly one-third of whom (32%) prioritize the freedom to take risks in their work as important to them, compared to an average of 25% among all generations. This risk, however, doesn't come without its angst. There are the associated fears of making the wrong career choice, disappointing parents and those closest to them. According to our FRAMES research, 45% of Millennials feel judged by older adults for their life choices. For Christian twentysomethings, there's the added dimension of wondering what God thinks of their choices and if their decisions are part of God's will for them. Yet, with all these concerns, these young adults are pioneering the reinvention of many concepts, including the concept of career. They are paving a new way of approaching work, holding out for a work-life mix that integrates how they play and work.

Hyper-Connected
and Relationally Confused

If you ask a Millennial what makes their generation unique, chances are their answer will have something to do with technology.[20] Nearly one-quarter of Millennials (24%) identified the use of technology as the distinctive characteristic of their generation, and 62% like that they know more about technology than older adults. Undoubtedly, this fluency with technology has revolutionized the way Millennials engage with the world and the information they have at their fingertips.

Access to information and networks has made for a more aware and tolerant generation. Millennials are more likely to celebrate racial and ethnic diversity.[21] They are increasingly accepting of homosexual lifestyles and nontraditional living arrangements.[22] This access to information also makes for a more socially conscious generation. Millennials believe sharing content is a form of advocacy and will use their networks to disseminate

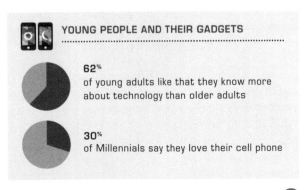

YOUNG PEOPLE AND THEIR GADGETS

62%
of young adults like that they know more about technology than older adults

30%
of Millennials say they love their cell phone

information about causes they are passionate about. But arguably, it's the sphere of the relationship that has been most affected by their enthusiastic embrace of technology.

Volumes have been written about the influence of technology and social networking on twentysomethings. Having grown up in the Internet era, young adults are digital natives, technologically fluent and globally connected. Much of their lives has been documented publicly on various iterations of the day's most popular social networking sites — Xanga, MySpace, Facebook, Google+, Twitter, Instagram, YouTube, Path, and Tumblr. According to FRAMES research, eight in ten Millennials have a profile on Facebook, and one-third are on Twitter and Instagram. A full 20% have posted a video of themselves online.[23] Even the way Millennials approach career networking has been revolutionized with the advent of LinkedIn.

The Dark Side of Social Media

While social media applications such as Facebook, Twitter, and Instagram have allowed Millennials to effortlessly expand their friend circles, this unceasing flow of very public relational connectedness can have a dark side. This is the first generation that has had to deal with the realities of cyber-bullying and cyber-stalking. In the face of rampant community-mindedness, many twentysomethings feel suffocated and saturated by fragmented and superficial relationships.

What Millennials may have in breadth, they often lack in depth. Whereas an average Millennial may have hundreds of "friends" on Facebook, the vast majority of these relationships are and will remain superficial. In presenting a public image, users of social networking sites often selectively post updates and pictures of positive events, leaving their viewers with a totally unrealistic, one-dimensional view of who they actually are.

Seeing all the "awesome" things "friends" are doing every day on Facebook can make one feel isolated, unaccomplished, and envious. Millennials are twice as likely to think their friends online are better off than they are as opposed to worse off when it comes to finances, status, prestige, and career. Many end up feeling like a "loser" as they sit alone at home, browsing through pictures of revelers on vacation, diners at a gourmet restaurant, or volunteers in exotic parts of the world. At the very least, not wanting to be judged or appear like a loser, the viewer may feel pressured to limit what he or she shares online, leading to the expression of only a fragmented version of his or her true self.

During my time as a chaplain at Princeton University, I saw firsthand the dark side of social media. Sarah was a junior when she approached me during my office hours. While talking with this young woman who was lonely, depressed, and overwhelmed, it took me only a few minutes to realize she was struggling with deep-seated self-esteem issues that were heavily exacerbated by her addiction to social media sites like Facebook and Instagram. To put it succinctly, she was suffering from FOMO, shorthand for "fear of missing out." When you spend too much time surfing the Internet, the dark side of YOLO becomes FOMO. The fear of missing out and feeling alone is certainly not unique to this generation, but the hyper-relational connectivity that social media has created has significantly compounded this anxiety. In the past, the occasional conversation would make you evaluate your life in the light of another, but now these conversations are being had dozens of times each week.

Sarah had hundreds of "friends" on Facebook, and the more profiles and status updates she browsed, the worse she felt about herself. As she sat alone in her dorm room, she could navigate through pictures of ex-boyfriends on spring break and postings by friends congratulating one another on academic honors or job offers. Status updates trumpeted the accomplishments of others, and she could feel her own sense of worth deflating with every new post. Even though she knew it was an unhealthy obsession, she couldn't stop logging on multiple times a day. It seemed to her that she alone was left out of the exciting adventures and meaningful relationships everyone else was constantly enjoying.

Ironically, Sarah also agonized over what pictures to upload to her own profile, likely perpetuating the cycle of FOMO for others. And even as she contemplated what pictures or comments to post, she felt like a fraud, disassociated from her "true" self and presenting only what she deemed "cool" enough to make public. Although she was a well-liked and accomplished young woman in her own right, surfing these social media sites made Sarah feel alone and as if nobody knew who she truly was.

The New Dating Game

Of course, Sarah isn't alone in her struggles over how to reconcile her online persona with real-life relationships. Strikingly, even intimate bonds like that of the dating relationship are not immune to the dual impact of technology to simultaneously propel and depersonalize a relationship.

These days, relationships start and end at the speed of broadband Internet. Texting and instant messaging have replaced traditional in-person courtship rituals. Dating doesn't start with a conversation; instead, it starts with virtual stalking: checking out friends, relatives, past relationships, hometowns, academic credentials, where the person likes to eat, and what they wore for Halloween last year. Google has made it easy to discover random trivia and sometimes deeply personal information about someone before ever actually having to spend any face-to-face time together. Even if someone doesn't have permission to view another's personal information, in our hyper-connected world they most likely know someone who wouldn't mind giving them access.

In addition to all this readily accessible information floating in cyberspace, there's been a proliferation of online dating sites like Match, ChristianMingle, and eHarmony, to name a few. These Internet companies have enabled those looking for romance to dip into a previously unimaginably expansive dating pool. In fact in a 2008 press release, eHarmony claimed that its service accounted for 2% of new US marriages. [24] For the busy, over-scheduled Millennial who doesn't have time to get out to meet new people, online dating services have opened up possibilities never experienced by any generation.

In theory this sounds great, yet the impersonal nature of the Internet often leaves the user with a random list of names based on what feels like a laundry list of vague interests. You can be sure that for every "successful" match made by one of these sites, there are thousands of people who feel even more isolated and alone after a failed attempt at a connection.

Despite the difficulties of navigating relationships in a murky virtual world, Millennials remain optimistic about the role technology can play in enriching their lives. Three-quarters of Millennials claim technology makes life easier, and 54% think it has the ability to bring people closer together.[25] Statistics like this highlight how Millennials positively view the impact of technology on their relationships.

The Internet facilitates the ability to connect to others with common interests in a way that previously never existed. The anonymity of online chat rooms and blogging sites may embolden troubled young adults to share intimate information they might feel uncomfortable or ashamed of sharing in person. In fact, in contrast with Millennials like Sarah, some young adults feel they can safely express their true selves only online. I remember reading the blog posts of former students who anonymously shared all their struggles online, but would never say a peep about these issues and concerns to their friends. For such Millennials, the

Internet allows them to live "authentically," providing the freedom and safety to speak honestly.

Delaying Marriage

While ministering to young professionals in New York City, I have officiated at more than my fair share of weddings. Over the years, however, I have noticed a trend among my congregation that reflects a broader generational trend: Young adults are putting off getting married. In fact, one of my first counseling experiences in the city was to work with a young couple who were living together and had questions about whether marriage was right for them.

Taylor and Brandon were well-educated young professionals who had been living together for several years. Although they were interested in getting married, Taylor came from a family of divorced parents, and as she put it, she viewed living together as a way to avoid the mistakes her parents made by ensuring she and Brandon were truly compatible for the long term. Both Taylor and Brandon felt "committed" to one another, but neither wanted to actually wed until they were further along in their careers, had saved enough money to feel financially stable, and felt strongly enough that their potential marriage would be a lasting one.

Statistics reveal many Millennials share this approach to marriage. Growing up in families where divorce is common, twentysomethings have felt forced to adapt the nature of their relationships in response to the seeming instability of the institution of marriage, and their view of marriage has evolved. Marriage and family formation have long been seen as rites of passage necessary in one's transition to adulthood, but this generation isn't quite ready to take that step. According to the US Census Bureau, the median age for a first marriage is the highest it has ever been in US history at 28.7 for men and 26.5 for women.[26] Marriage rates for twentysomethings are the lowest they have ever been. Only 21% of Millennials are married, which is half the rate of their parents' generation at the same life stage.[27]

Young adults do want to get married; more than eight in ten say they want to be married *at some point*. They just aren't ready *yet* and only about a quarter (28%) would consider it a top goal for their twenties. And, honestly, older generations are okay with this — in fact, they seem to be encouraging Millennials to wait. Only 13% of Boomers think marriage should be a top priority for twentysomethings. And, while only 10% of Millennials think young people are waiting too long to

---

FUTURE FAMILY   *among 18- to 29-year-olds

I want to be married at some point: **82%**

I feel well equipped to be a good spouse in the future: **40%**

I want to be a parent at some point: **77%**

I feel well equipped to be a good parent in the future: **36%**

get married these days, that's actually twice as many as Boomers (5%).

So why delay marriage? It is not merely symptomatic of a generation's desire for prolonged adolescence. Several factors contribute to this trend of delayed marriage, reflecting a growing cultural pragmatism when it comes to marriage.

Test-Driving the Relationship

Skeptical of another faltering institution, Millennials essentially want to "test-drive" relationships before engaging in the commitment of marriage. They haven't given up on the concept of marriage, but they are cautious. This attitude is understandable given that almost 40% of Millennials did not grow up in two-parent homes.[28] With divorce rates climbing toward the 50% mark in the 1970s and 1980s, Millennials are all too aware of the financial and emotional consequences of failed marriages, many having witnessed the disintegration of this pivotal relationship firsthand. With fears of divorce lurking close behind dreams of wedding vows, many twentysomethings have chosen to delay marriage and focus instead on developing themselves personally and professionally and on pursuing long-term dating relationships so they can get to know their partners well.[29]

The delay in marriage has also been accompanied by an upsurge in acceptance of cohabitation. Nearly two-thirds of young adults (60%) agree it's a good idea to live together before you get married — substantially

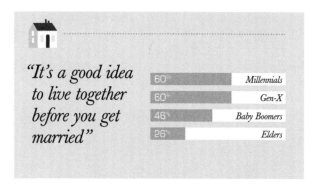

"It's a good idea to live together before you get married"

60%	Millennials
60%	Gen-X
46%	Baby Boomers
26%	Elders

more than their parents and grandparents believe. In the same way they would engage in thorough research before making a major purchase, many twentysomethings feel they owe it to themselves to explore their options before they make a major life commitment. Much like Taylor and Brandon, many Millennials believe living together before marriage is a key step in avoiding divorce and finding marital success.

Prioritizing Career

With the rates of twentysomethings seeking higher education at an all-time high, Millennials are delaying marriage and family formation to pursue education and career-related goals. I have found it common for many of the young adults I work with to prioritize their work life over their personal relationships. In fact, many young adults would scoff at prioritizing love as naive, unwise, or unambitious. In their list of things to do before turning thirty, young adults rank marriage far below finishing their education, starting a career, and pursuing their dreams. Millennials believe you need to "figure out who you are" before you marry someone else—seven in ten agree you should wait to get married until you are fully developed as a person.

A recent article in the *New York Times* discussed the phenomenon of college women engaging in casual hook-ups as a functional strategy enabling them to have enjoyable sex lives while focusing the bulk of their time and energy on their academic pursuits.[30] It has become commonplace for Millennials to find alternative means to enjoy intimate relationships outside of the bonds of matrimony.

Pursuing Financial Stability

Millennials' views on marriage are also not immune to the influences of a sluggish economy. With 69% of Millennials indicating one should be "well established financially" before getting married, financial instability among twentysomethings has been a significant factor in the delay of related rites of passage into adulthood. High unemployment rates and increasing amounts of student debt have contributed to a dearth of home and car ownership among young adults.

Even those Millennials who did not attend college, thereby avoiding educational loans, don't feel they are earning enough to be financially capable of providing for a family. Census data show that between 2006 and 2011, home ownership rates declined the most among households headed by twenty-five- to thirty-four-year-olds, dipping from 46.7% to 39.7%, while the number

IT'S **MY** LIFE

Parents and kids don't always agree on what's most important
in life – case in point, what Millennials think is most
important to do in your twenties and what Boomers think.

....

Financial independence
59%
72%

Finish education
52%
64%

Start your career
51%
64%

Find yourself
40%
47%

Follow your dreams
31%
33%

Become spiritually mature
29%
39%

Get married
28%
13%

Enjoy life
24%
30%

Have kids
21%
8%

Travel abroad
20%
15%

Serve the poor
9%
11%

Be in a serious relationship
9%
3%

Become famous/influential
5%
1%

Millennials   *Baby Boomers*

of renters increased by more than one million.[31] Money
that at one time may have gone toward a down payment
for a home is now being used to pay off student
loans. A recent study by the University of Michigan's
Transportation Research Institute found young adults
had the lowest rates of vehicle purchases in 2011,
with those over seventy-five and above purchasing cars
at a higher rate than twentysomethings.[32] But some
economists theorize that while rates of home and car
ownership are currently low, they remain valued long-
term goals for Millennials as the economy improves.[33]

Moving Back with the Parents

Notably, more Millennials than ever have moved back
in with their parents. In 2012, approximately 36% of
young adults ages eighteen to thirty-one were living
at their parents' home, the highest number in this age
group in four decades.[34] Many of these young adults
who are said to have "boomeranged" back home
have chosen to do so because they are unemployed or
enrolled in college and simply can't afford a place of
their own in a difficult economy.

Predictably, the majority of these young adults are
unmarried. But many Millennials aren't simply gritting
their teeth and returning home against their wills.
Relatively few Millennials (25%) or their parents (17%)
now consider "financial independence" a key marker
of adulthood. And what may surprise many is that this
generation of twentysomethings generally has close and
mutually supportive relationships with their parents.
Although there are, of course, many exceptions to this,

Millennials overall appear to view their parents as a positive influence in their lives, seeking their advice and guidance. Multigenerational living arrangements are more prevalent and are often seen as being not only beneficial but enjoyable.

For some, seeing a young adult still living with their parents is a sign of immaturity on the part of the child and the unhealthy coddling on the part of the parents, but for Megan and her parents, moving back home was an unexpected opportunity. Megan was a college graduate who had started a two-year internship at a small New York City nonprofit start-up, while taking classes towards her master's degree in teaching. Because she couldn't afford to pay rent for a studio apartment, Megan did what many of her peers have done: She moved back home to live with her parents. Although she was initially apprehensive about moving back in with them, she was pleasantly surprised to find her relationship with them grew stronger. She viewed her time at home as "an unexpected blessing," reasoning that once she was married, she would never get to live with her parents again. Additionally, she was able to save up some money, which she used to contribute to the household utilities and to treat her parents to the occasional fancy dinner or Broadway show. For Megan and her supportive parents, they cherished her two years back at home as their last chance to live together as a family.

Given all these factors, it's easy to see why Millennials haven't readily embraced the institution of marriage, but there are some good reasons to be optimistic about their views on marriage and family. Millennials report that their two top priorities in life are "being a good parent" and "having a successful marriage."[35] Despite the low rates of married twentysomethings, marriage — and ultimately parenthood — are still highly valued in this generation.

Although Millennials feel they must postpone entering into marriage until they are more financially stable and have achieved their own personal and career goals, marriage is still a perceived goal by many young adults. Millennials also still see value in having children in the context of a family. In fact, Millennials are unexpectedly "old-fashioned" when it comes to their views on child rearing: 63% of surveyed twentysomethings disapprove of having children outside of marriage, slightly higher than their parents and grandparents and lower than Gen Xers. More than three-quarters of Millennials who are not parents hope to have children in the future. Given all these statistics, perhaps twentysomethings are delaying marriage not because they have a low view of

"It's not that important to be married to someone before you have kids together"

37%	*Millennials*
39%	*Gen-X*
28%	*Baby Boomers*
23%	*Elders*

it; rather, because they value marriage so much, they're willing to push it off to increase the likelihood of a successful marriage.

The Time of Your Life

If after reading this short book, you find yourself disagreeing with much of it, you're probably a Millennial, and you've just proven my point (sarcastic humor intended). Twentysomethings are hard to pin down, and I hope the previous pages have given some insight into the context of what has shaped this particular generation. What I do want to make clear is that with all the statistics presented in this FRAME, no one mold explains what defines any generation. With that said, I have articulated *hope* and *change* as two words that seem to be characteristic of the current twentysomethings. Their optimism is amazing and energizing, and I feel quite fortunate to have spent much of my work life intimately involved with them.

I see the way Millennials are creatively using and developing technology to address so much of what they see as broken in this world. It is absolutely staggering to think about what this generation will be able to accomplish. They are eager to use all that is unique about this period of history to advance social causes and address social ills. This is deeply encouraging. Yet, my concerns grow when I look at the limitations of technology.

What technology will never be able to change is the disposition of the human heart in its potential for good and evil. With all the brokenness this generation has witnessed, will they be naive about the nature of the human heart, or will they wrestle with the ever-present reality of human greed, anger, violence, and pride that brought about all they've dramatically experienced? Where will they anchor their hopes for this kind of deeper change?

If ultimately the hope of this generation is grounded upon merely hard work and technological advances, Millennials will have overlooked the lessons history so often teaches regarding human nature and our capacity for self-destruction. As with every generation, our deepest hopes for change have to be grounded not in human potential, but in divine grace that has been assured by the gospel of Jesus Christ. As simplistic as it may sound, the gospel alone has the profound power to change not only human hearts, but relationships, and larger societal structures and institutions that arise from these relationships. My prayer is that this generation would take hold of this gospel hope and explore its intersection with the world in which they live, work, love, and play. I hope they will apply their entrepreneurial spirit to discover in ways that previous generations have not how the gospel applies to new aspects of our complex, multi-cultural, pluralistic society.

In many respects, Jesus is the ultimate Millennial. He defies all those who would try to label him. He is the paragon of refusing to give up hope for change even in the midst of the gravest evil. Christ had a passion for change as evidenced by his willingness to suffer and die on a cross so we would have a hope that is certain. It is this hope anchored in Christ that will provide for this generation the most profound expression of all that is good, creative, authentic, and lovely about them.

I hope the church will be able to understand what makes this generation so similar and dissimilar to previous generations, and learn how to communicate and entrust the gospel to them. If this generation were able to grasp the gospel in its transforming power, I am confident they would appropriate it in ways this world has yet to realize. This possibility excites me to no end.

Even though I am not a Millennial, I too am very hopeful. I have worked with enough twentysomethings to know the tremendous possibility and visionary potential of this generation. I admire their determination to have a life that is whole and integrated, where work and rest and play are intertwined. I don't know if it is possible to combine all of this together, but I am confident that if any generation can, the Millennials will figure out a way. I hope to live long enough to see the legacy of this intriguing generation and to see the world they will pass on to future generations. ◆

20 AND SOMETHING

Have the Time of Your Life (And Figure It All Out Too)

RE/FRAME

BY PHYLLIS TICKLE

The "quarter-life crisis" is a contemporary turn of phrase many twentysomethings use to describe a human affliction that is, in fact, far older. Our forebearers would have simply called it "the lack of a center."

In American Westernized culture, and especially in these current turbulent times of ours, a primary preoccupation in one's twenties is to find one's center. For this center—or lack thereof—will become the foundation on which one builds a life, ready or not.

Once upon a time, such an exercise was easy, because your center was an inherited given. People were born into a particular context—their parents' city or town, which would almost inevitably become their city or town as an adult. In effect, a person's physical rootedness in a place of origin *was* his or her psychological center—he or she married within it, found gainful work within or through it, procreated by means of it, added to it, and then passed it on. It was the American way of life.

But the Industrial Revolution began the shredding of that fabric of surety. Then, less than two centuries later, the horror of the world's first truly global war completed that process of rifting and tearing. My own generation, born in the Great Depression and reared in catastrophic war, became the first American generation to mature, en masse, in the midst of altered marrying patterns and the displacement from the towns that had been our parents' constancy. As we came of age, the world shifted beneath our feet.

Our diversified education, wider breadth of knowledge,

expanded employment opportunities, and heightened international awareness all converged in a cascade of interruptions to the way things had always been.

A centered identity was no longer guaranteed for us. But then you—the Millennials—came along. And we watched as the fabric of certainty deteriorated altogether. All our coming-of-age challenges cannot compare to your generation's hurdles of delayed marriage and optional parenthood, changed gender roles and expectations, morphing vocations and constantly evolving requirements in skill sets, transience even within the circle of one's closest friends, lack of respite from at times intrusive electronic stimulation, and more. Indeed, the "givens" of twentieth-century life have been swept away within the last two or three decades of Westernized experience. Geo-sociopolitical loyalties—like family, career, friendship, location—are no longer ensured, and an easy or natural cohesion is no longer possible. Yet like a whirlpool in its rushing, we cannot *be*—not without our center. Where to look? Where to find it?

A century ago, some wise and kindly soul would have said, "Find your center in the church." But for several decades now, each and every use of the term *church* has grown increasingly complex and even confusing. As a word, *church* now contains multiple meanings.

Yet it is in the honest wrestling toward a useful definition of church that we can find, even in today's turbulence, that some sureties do and will hold.

I know. I did my own wrestling in my time. In

retrospect, it was easier than it may be today for you, in the midst of your increasingly complex and accelerated pace of life. But for all of us, the fact remains: We need constants that are not subject to shifts and changes. We need a center. And wrapped within the narratives and praxis and ageless traditions of the church, we find it.

I'm not talking about church polity or ecclesial form and structure. These are temporal houses we have built to make safe the space between us and the Source from which we come and to which we, by grace, shall return. They are the buffer of institutional distance that allows a culture to have formative and productive conversation with the sacred, but they are not centering places themselves, nor are they fixed points. By their very nature, they will shift according to the time to fulfill their purpose. But the narratives and the praxis and the traditions do not. And where the "givens" of former life have been shaken, these have not.

If you can pass through these externals of the church, its structure and politics, then you are ready to discover the centering function of church that anchors the life we are charged with living.

For some, this centering may be quiet retreat or studied pilgrimage from time to time. For others, it is the observance of Sabbath, the discipline of fasting, the alignment of one's life with the liturgical year, or the commitment to unflinching tithing.

For me, none of these became the center, though each of them has played a role in my time as a Christian. Rather, it was — and is — the keeping of the daily offices of prayer that, from the time of my own wandering twenties until these years of my early eighties, has held.

Some call it fixed-hour prayer or observing the hours. By any of its names, it is an ancient tradition of Judaism and of Christianity. It is the pause, every three hours of the day from sunup to bedtime, to pray the prayers that have been appointed for that day and hour by the church from her very beginning. It is to step briefly into the invisible and vibrant church of all our fellow Christians within one's time zone who are also stopped for those few minutes to praise and glorify the Creator together, though we are physically apart. It is, at its conclusion, the sure knowledge that the prayers just offered will be offered again within another fifty-some minutes by fellow Christians in the next time zone. And again after that, in the next, and again in the next.

And so it goes, creating a constant cascade of prayer before the throne of God. It is also, because the prayers are the psalms and/or drawn from the ancient prayers of the early church fathers, the melding, however briefly, with the church universal, as she has always been and shall be so long as time itself holds.

Observing the hours may not be your discipline, of course. You may require a different centering pole for building a life. But somewhere within the rich narratives and praxes and traditions of our faith, there is the stake that is yours.

It is easy to get distracted by the externals of any institution, including the church. But beyond them, we find our center—the place where Christ meets us in the midst of all our unknowns, our turbulence, our shifting certainties. And that is the center we need — whether you're twentysomething or eightysomething. ◆

. . . .

Phyllis Tickle is the founding editor of the Religion Department of *Publishers Weekly* and a noted author and essayist. Her most recent books are the best-selling *The Great Emergence, Emergence Christianity*, and *The Words of Jesus — A Gospel of the Sayings of Our Lord.*

AFTER YOU READ

- What about the Millennial experience described in this book resonated most with you and your experiences?

- What qualities of young adults would you most praise? Is there something that makes you urge caution?

- After reading this, would you agree young adults today are different from previous generations? Why or why not?

- In what ways do you see twentysomethings around you channeling hope and change?

- If young adults are looking for a grand vision to embrace, why do you think the church has failed to capture their imagination?

- Do you agree with Phyllis Tickle's contention that one must find a center? How could finding your center within the church impact your own faith life?

- Do you resonate with any of Phyllis's suggestions for finding a center: a retreat, observing the Sabbath, fasting, aligning with the liturgical year, tithing, or fixed-hour prayer?

● Phyllis Tickle is, as this book is published, entering her eightieth year of life. Her wisdom, though, speaks across the gap of decades. When have you seen intergenerational mentorship work best? Would you be willing to engage someone of another generation in a mutually beneficial mentoring relationship?

SHARE THIS FRAME

Who else needs to know about this trend?
Here are some tools to engage with others.

SHARE THE BOOK
- Any one of your friends can sample a FRAME for FREE.
  Visit zondervan.com/ShareFrames to learn how.

- Know a ministry, church, or small group that would benefit
  from reading this FRAME? Contact your favorite bookseller, or
  visit Zondervan.com/buyframes for bulk purchasing information.

SHARE THE VIDEOS
- See videos for all 9 FRAMES on barnaframes.com and use
  the share links to post them on your social networks and share
  them with friends.

SHARE ON FACEBOOK
- Like facebook.com/barnaframes and be the first to see new
  videos, discounts, and updates from the Barna FRAMES team.

SHARE ON TWITTER
- Start following @barnaframes and stay current with the
  trends that are influencing and changing our culture.

- Join the conversation and include #barnaframes whenever
  you post a FRAMES related idea or culture-shaping trend.

SHARE ON INSTAGRAM
- Follow instagram.com/barnaframes for sharable visual
  posts and infographics that will keep you in the know.

Barna Group

 ZONDERVAN°

ABOUT THE RESEARCH

FRAMES started with the idea that people need simple, clear ideas to live more meaningful lives in the midst of increasingly complex times. To help make sense of culture, each FRAME includes major public opinion studies conducted by Barna Group.

If you're into the details, you'll want to know the research behind the *20 and Something* FRAME included one thousand surveys conducted among a representative sample of adults over the age of eighteen living in the United States and included an oversample of 404 interviews completed by eighteen- to twenty-nine-year-olds. This survey was conducted from June 25, 2013, through July 1, 2013. The sampling error for both surveys is plus or minus 3 percentage points, at the 95% confidence level.

If you're really into the research details, find more at www.barnaframes.com.

ABOUT BARNA GROUP

In its thirty-year history, Barna Group has conducted more than one million interviews over the course of hundreds of studies and has become a go-to source for insights about faith and culture. Currently led by David Kinnaman, Barna Group's vision is to provide people with credible knowledge and clear thinking, enabling them to navigate a complex and changing culture. The company was started by George and Nancy Barna in 1984.

Barna Group has worked with thousands of businesses, nonprofit organizations, and churches across the country, including many Protestant and Catholic congregations and denominations. Some of its clients have included the American Bible Society, CARE, Compassion, Easter Seals, Habitat for Humanity, NBC Universal, the Salvation Army, Walden Media, the ONE Campaign, SONY, Thrivent, US AID, and World Vision.

The firm's studies are frequently used in sermons and talks. And its public opinion research is often quoted in major media outlets, such as *CNN, USA Today*, the *Wall Street Journal*, Fox News, *Chicago Tribune*, the *Huffington Post,* the *New York Times, Dallas Morning News*, and the *Los Angeles Times*.

Learn more about Barna Group at www.barna.org.

THANKS

....

Even small books take enormous effort.

First, thanks go to David H. Kim for his well-articulated and cohesive work on this FRAME—offering his experiences, observations, and years of counseling twentysomethings to create what we pray is a prophetic and illuminating look at how life in this formative decade is changing.

We are also incredibly grateful for the contribution of Phyllis Tickle, who we knew would offer us wisdom both winsome and tested. And, of course, she did.

Next, Barna Group gratefully acknowledges the efforts of the team at HarperCollins Christian Publishing, especially Chip Brown and Melinda Bouma for catching the vision from the get-go. Others at HarperCollins who have made huge contributions include Jennifer Keller, Kate Mulvaney, Mark Sheeres, and Shari Vanden Berg.

The FRAMES team at Barna Group consists of Elaina Buffon, Bill Denzel, Traci Hochmuth, Pam Jacob, Clint Jenkin, Robert Jewe, David Kinnaman, Jill Kinnaman, Elaine Klautzsch, Stephanie Smith, and Roxanne Stone. Bill and Stephanie consistently made magic out of thin air. Clint and Traci brought the research to life—along with thoughtful analysis from Ken Chitwood. And

Roxanne deserves massive credit as a shaping force on FRAMES. Amy Duty did heroic work on FRAMES designs, from cover to infographics.

Finally, others who have had a huge role in bringing FRAMES to life include Brad Abare, Justin Bell, Jean Bloom, Patrick Dodd, Grant England, Esther Fedorkevich, Josh Franer, Jane Haradine, Aly Hawkins, Kelly Hughes, Steve McBeth, Geof Morin, Jesse Oxford, Beth Shagene, and Santino Stoner.

Many thanks!

NOTES

1. "Millennials: A Portrait of Generation Next," Pew Research Center, 2010, http://www.pewsocialtrends.org/files/2010/10/Millennials-confident-connected-open-to-change.pdf.

2. Zach O'Malley Greenburg, "How Millennials Can Survive and Thrive in the New Economy," *Forbes*, November 16, 2011, http://www.forbes.com/sites/zackomalleygreenburg/2011/11/16/how-millennials-can-survive-and-thrive-in-the-new-economy/#.

3. "A Rising Share of Young Adults Live in Their Parents' Home," Pew Research Center (2013), http://www.pewsocialtrends.org/2013/08/01/a-rising-share-of-young-adults-live-in-their-parents-home/.

4. Ibid.

5. "Millennials: A Portrait," Pew Research.

6. Ibid.

7. "Conan O'Brien Delivers the 2011 Dartmouth Commencement Address," Team Coco (July 1, 2011), http://teamcoco.com/content/watch-conan-give-dartmouth-college-commencement-address.

8. Ibid.

9. Hadley Malcolm and Barbara Hansen, "Housing Recovery Leaves Millennials Behind," *USA Today*, July 18, 2013, http://www.usatoday.com/story/money/personalfinance/2013/07/17/young-adult-home-ownership-rates-decline/2456845/.

10. "Millennials: A Portrait," Pew Research.

11. Jeanne Meister, "Job Hopping Is the New Normal for Millennials," *Forbes*, August 14, 2012, http://www.forbes.com/sites/jeannemeister/2012/08/14/job-hopping-is-the-new-normal-for-millennials-three-ways-to-prevent-a-human-resource-nightmare/.

12. Cliff Zukin and Mark Szeltner, "Talent Report: What Workers Want in 2012," *Net Impact*, May 2012, http://netimpact.org/docs/publications-docs/talent-report-what-workers-want-in-2012-full-report.

13. Jason Notte, "Harvard Grads Wary of Wall Street," *MSN Money*, May 29, 2013, http://money.msn.com/now/post.aspx?post=70286011-9761-4805-94a7-246ca8a3399c.

14. Meister, "Job Hopping."

15. William Deresiewicz, "The Entrepreneurial Generation," *New York Times*, November 12, 2011, http://www.nytimes.com/2011/11/13/opinion/sunday/the-entrepreneurial-generation.html?pagewanted=all&_r=0.

16. Ibid.

17. Ibid.

18. "Millennials and the Future of Work," oDesk (April 23, 2013), http://www.slideshare.net/oDesk/millennials-and-the-future-of-work-survey-results.

19. Ibid.

20. "Millennials: A Portrait," Pew Research.

21. Ibid.

22. Ibid.

23. Ibid.

24. "eHarmony Study Finds an Average of 236 eHarmony Members Marry Every Day," Harris Interactive (July 28, 2008), http://www.eharmony.com/press-release/8/.

25. "Millennials: A Portrait," Pew Research.

26. Diana B. Elliot, "Figures: Historical Marriage Trends from 1890–2010," US Census Bureau (2011), http://www.census.gov/hhes/socdemo/marriage/data/acs/ElliottetalPAA2012figs.pdf.

27. "Millennials: A Portrait," Pew Research.

28. Ibid.

29. Eilene Zimmerman, "Modern Romance: Gen-Y Is Late to the Wedding, But Wants Romance," *Christian Science Monitor*, February 13, 2012, http://www.csmonitor.com/USA/Society/2012/0213/Modern-romance-Gen-Y-is-late-to-the-wedding-but-wants-marriage/(page)/5.

30. Kate Taylor, "Sex on Campus: She Can Play That Game, Too," *New York Times*, July 12, 2013, http://www.nytimes.com/2013/07/14/fashion/sex-on-campus-she-can-play-that-game-too.html?pagewanted=all&_r=0.

31. Malcolm and Hansen, "Housing Recovery."

32. Keith Naughton, "Boomers Replace Their Children as No. 1 Market for Autos," *Bloomberg News*, August 5, 2013, http://www.bloomberg.com/news/2013-08-05/automania-strikes-boomers-supplanting-kids-as-buyers.html.

33. Brad Tuttle, "The Great Debate: Do Millennials Really Want Cars, or Not?" *Time*, August 9, 2013, http://business.time.com/2013/08/09/the-great-debate-do-millennials-really-want-cars-or-not/.

34. "Parents' Home," Pew Research.

35. "Millennials: A Portrait," Pew Research.